Abstrabulous

Joyce L. Williams

Archway Publishing books may be ordered through booksellers or by contacting:

Archway Publishing
1663 Liberty Drive
Bloomington, IN 47403
www.archwaypublishing.com
844-669-3957

Interior Image Credit: Joyce L. Williams of JLW LIT Abstracts
www.jlwlitabstracts.com

ISBN: 978-1-6657-3749-4 (sc)
ISBN: 978-1-6657-3748-7 (e)

Print information available on the last page.

Archway Publishing rev. date: 2/16/2023

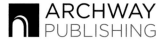

Abstrabulous

Artist's Originals

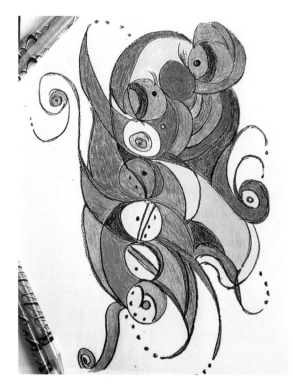

Bella's Beauty

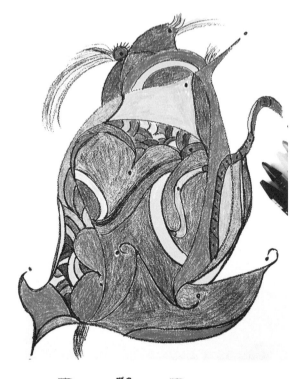

Dazzling Dance

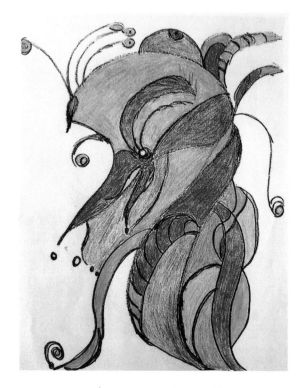

Elegant Beek

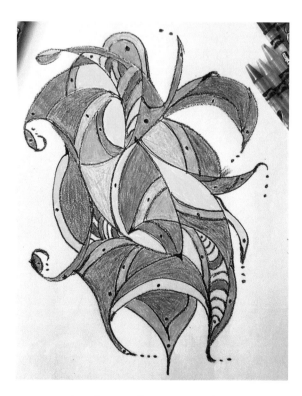

Majestic Motion

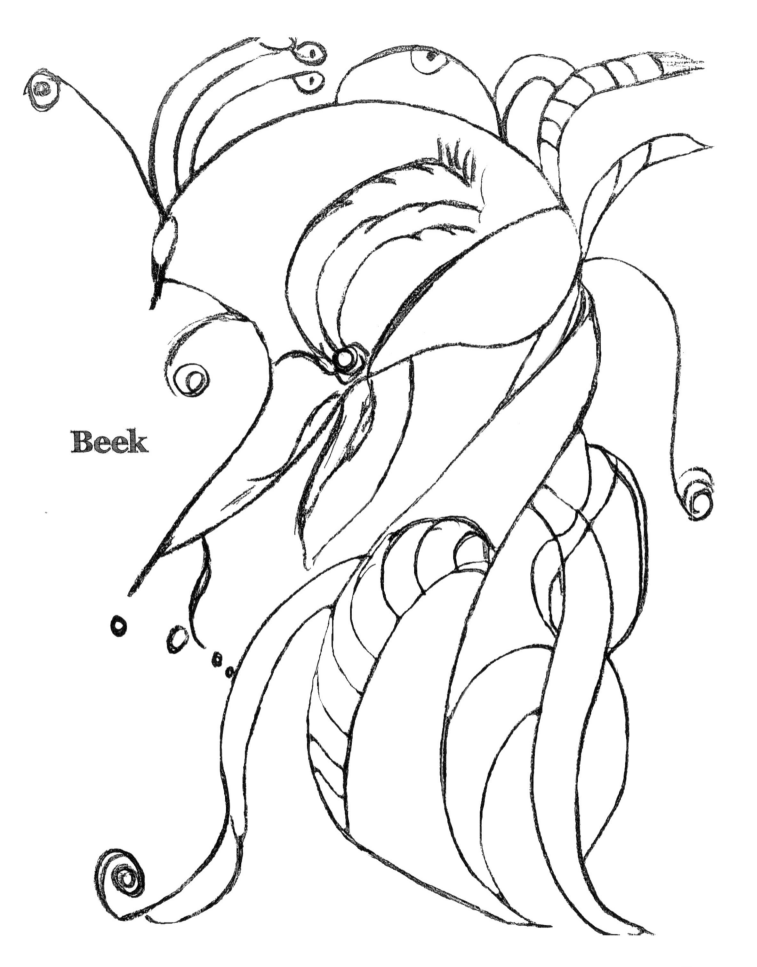

Beek

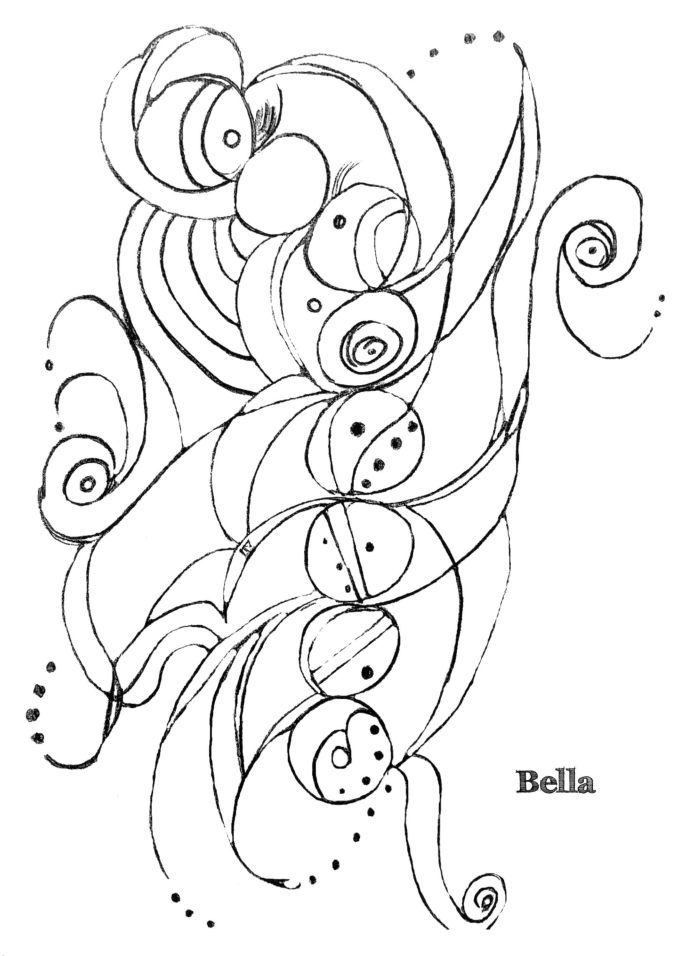

Bella

Bells

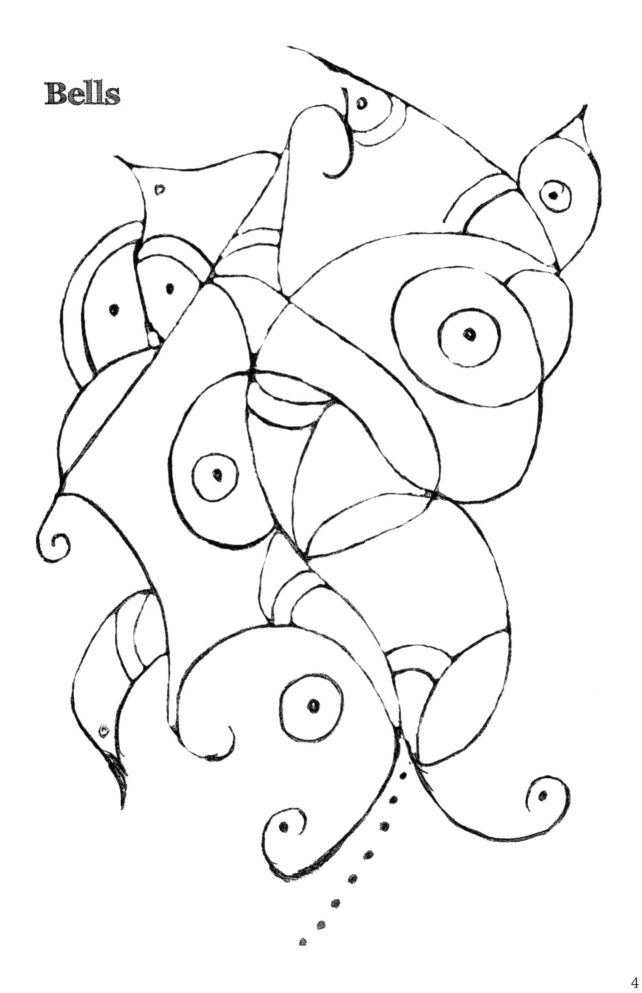

4

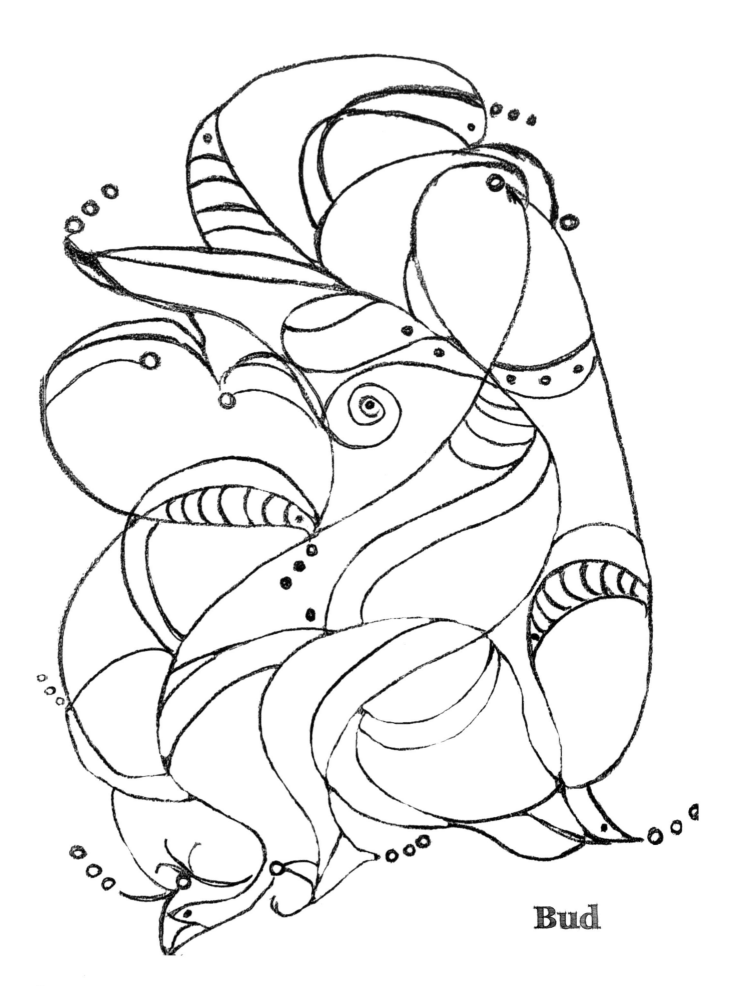

Bud

Curves

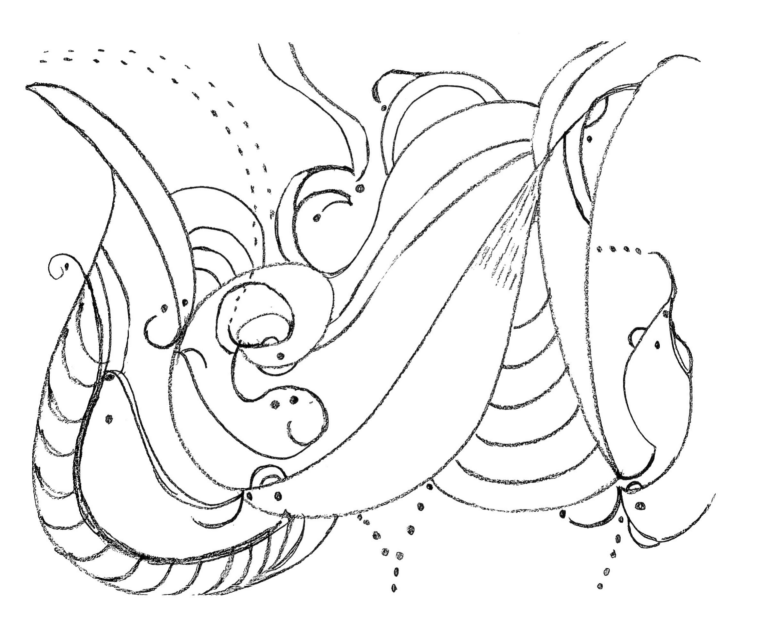

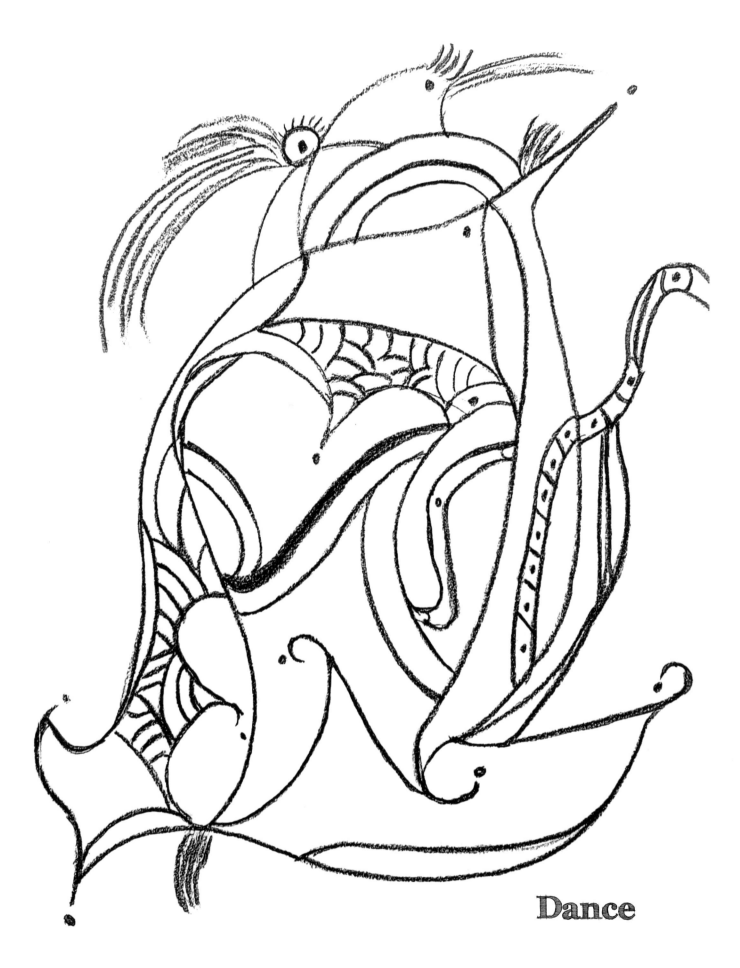

Dance

Desire

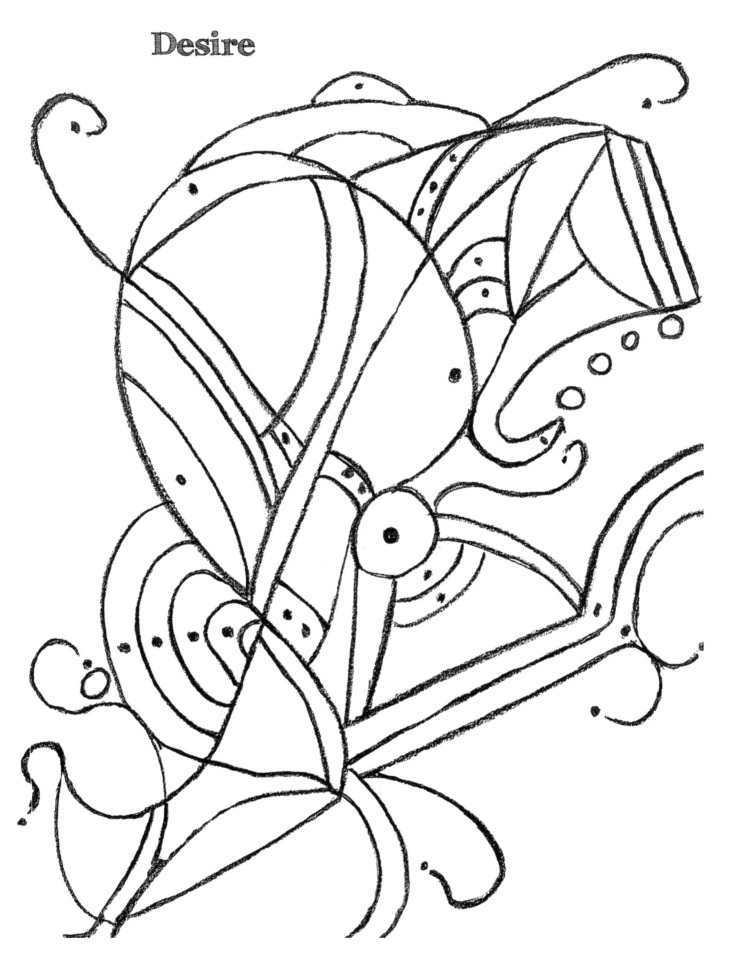

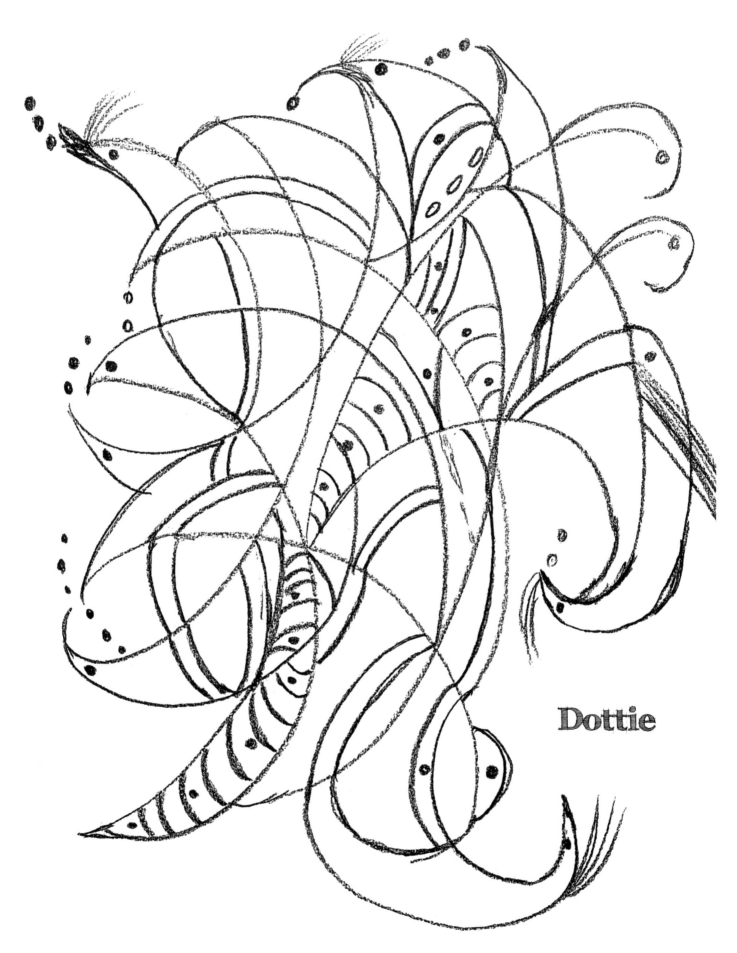

Dottie

Fancy

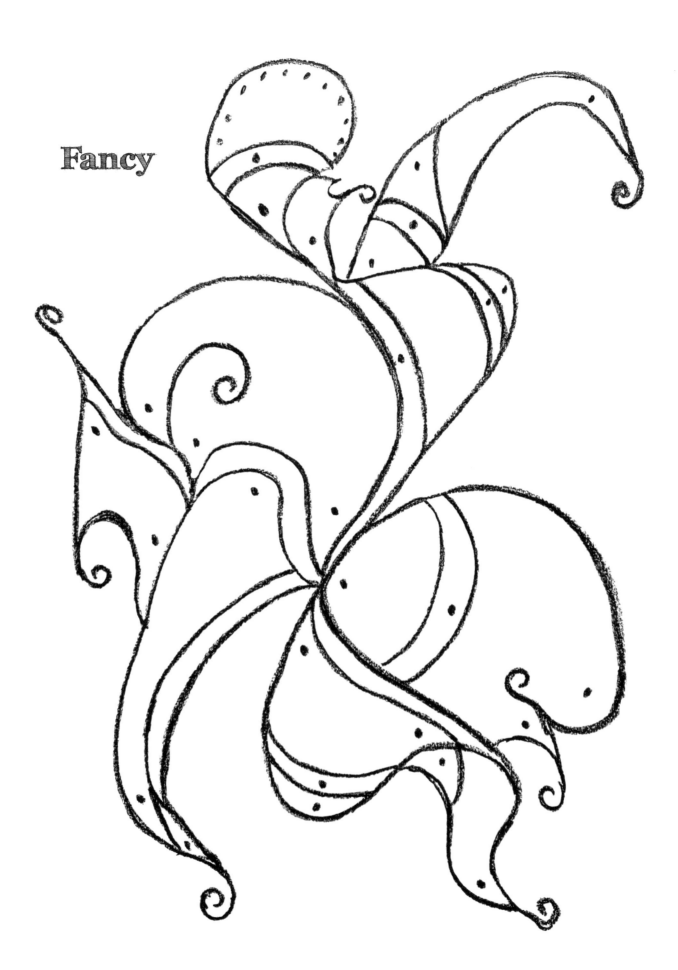

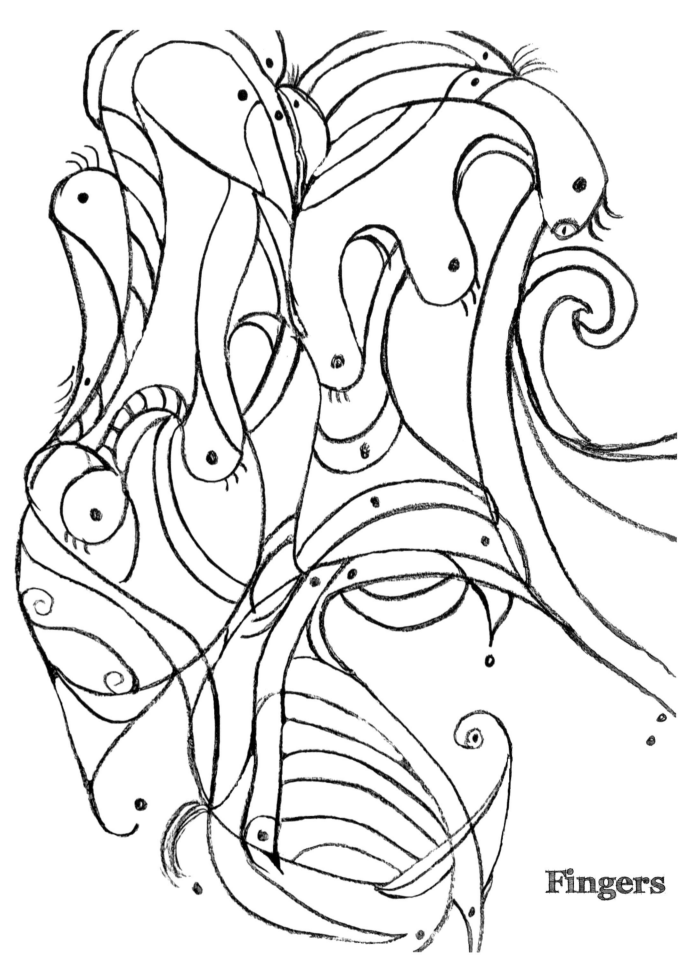

Fingers

Fiore

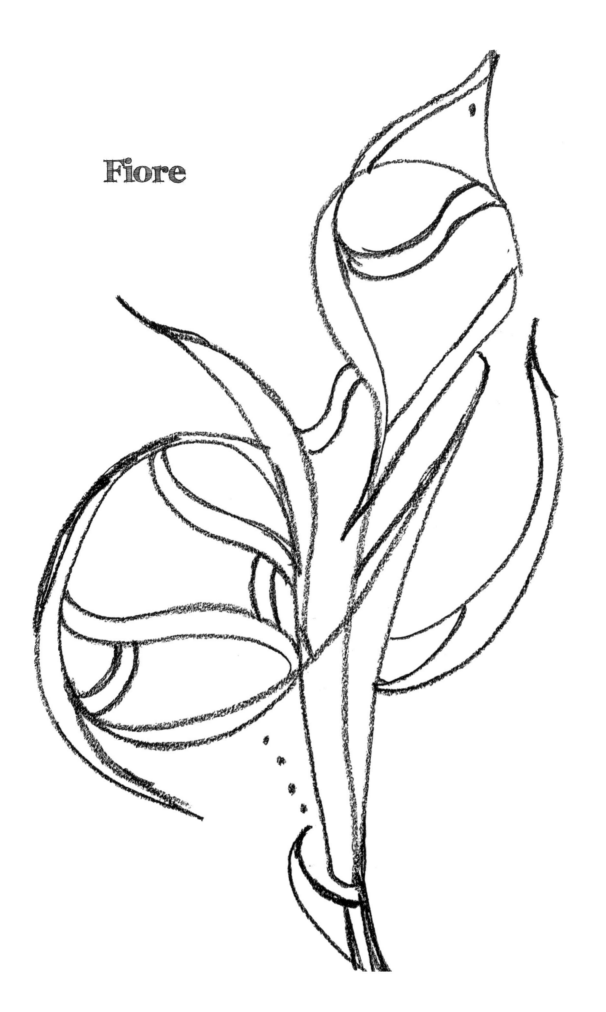

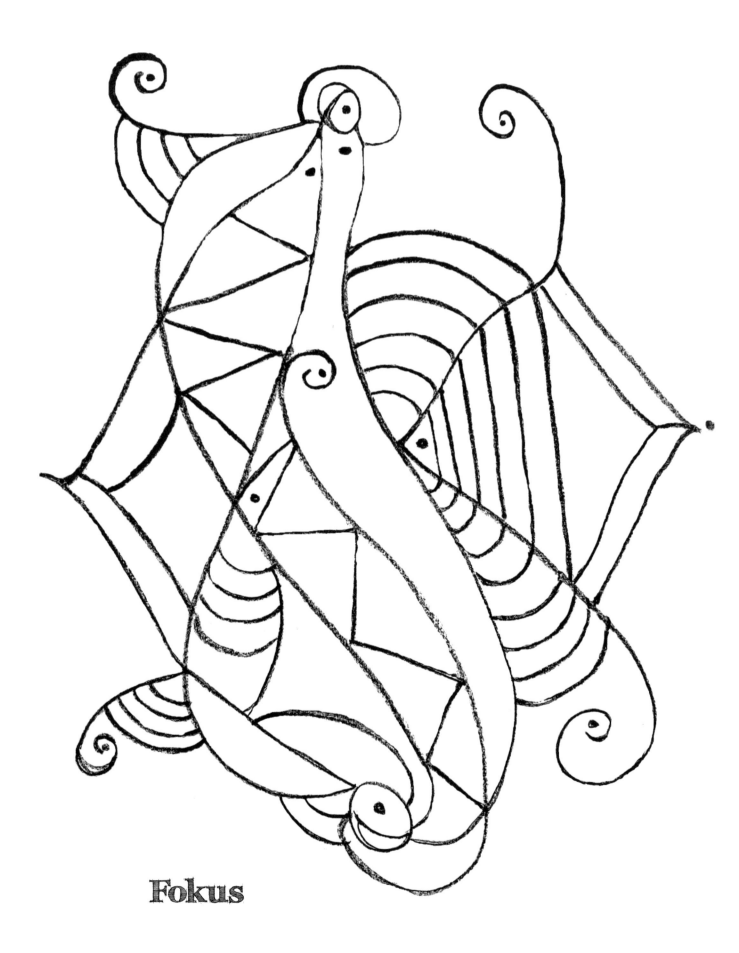

Fokus

13

Jefee

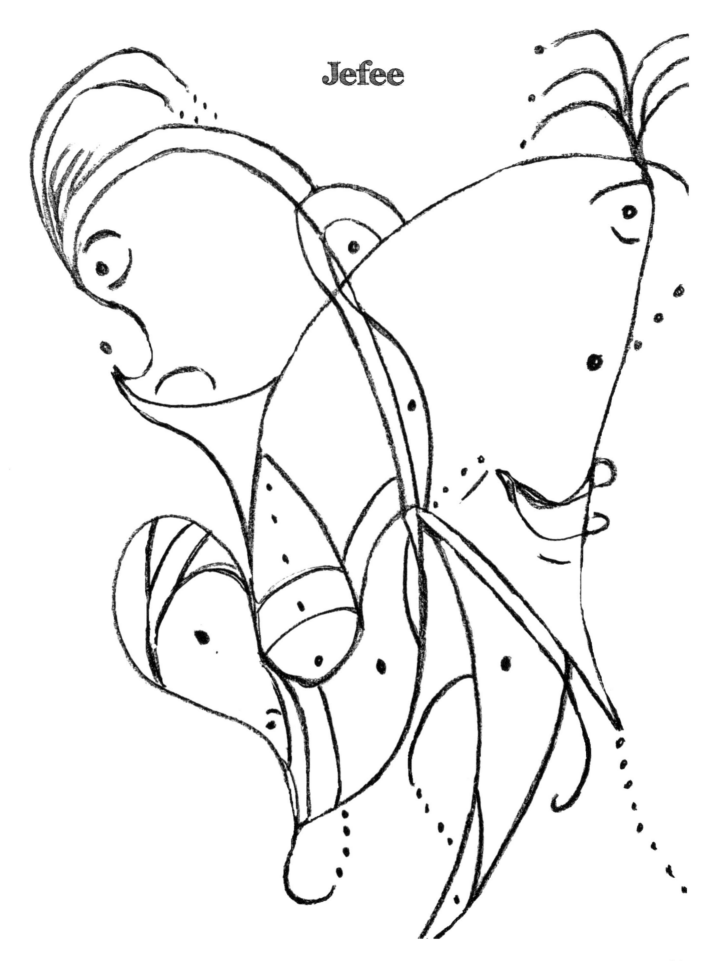

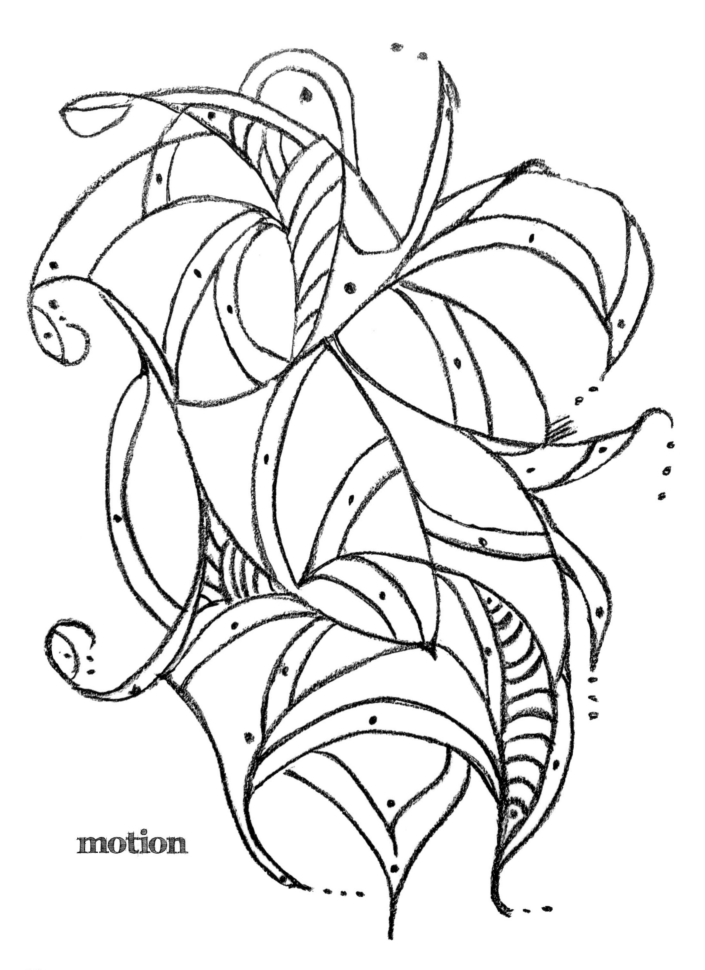

motion

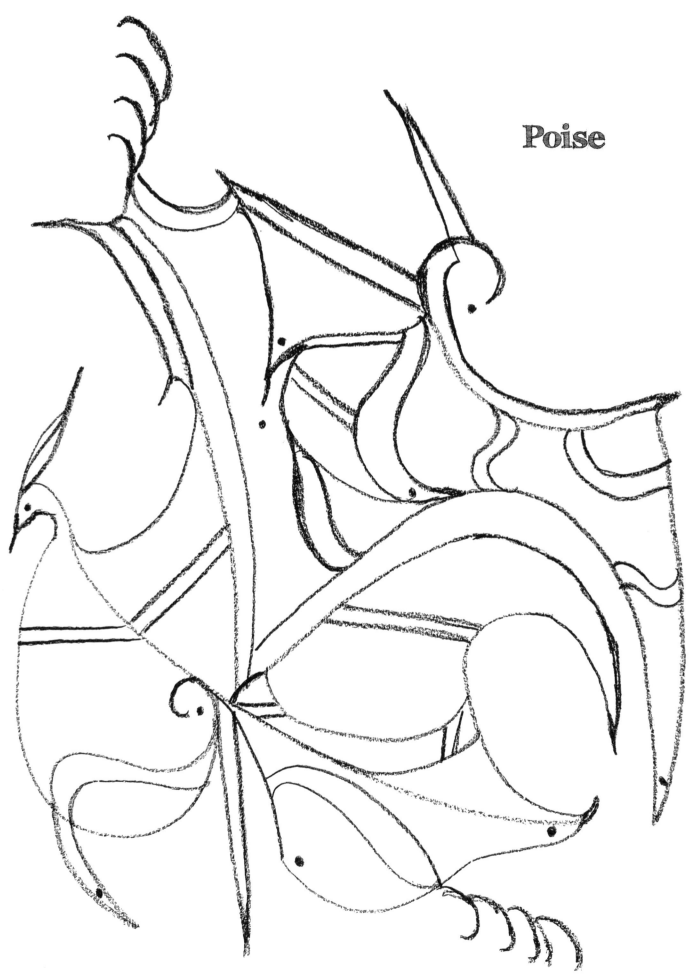

Poise

16

Purpose

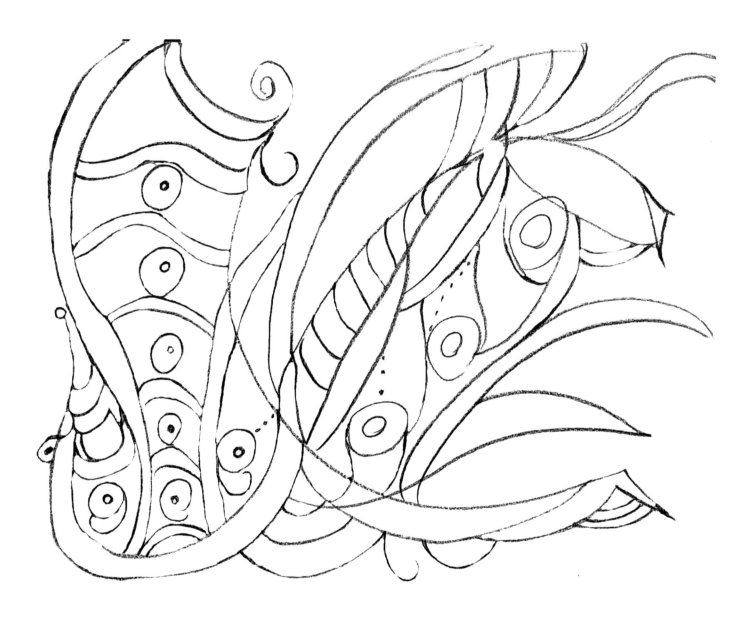

swirley

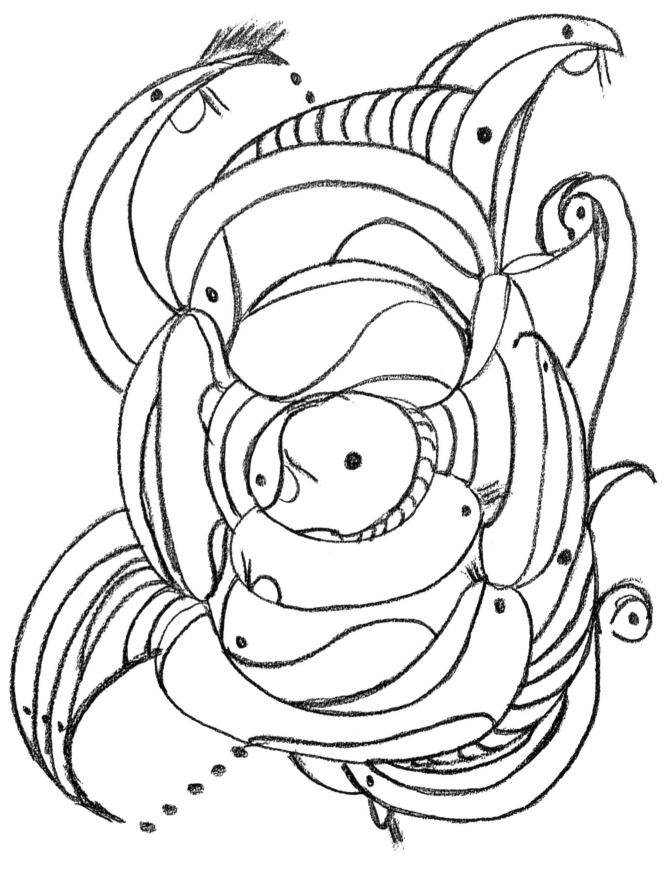

Woops

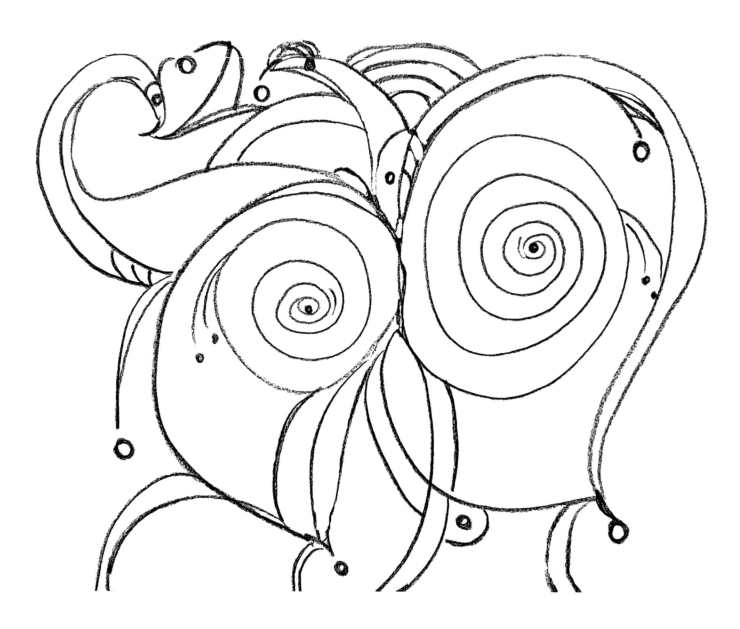

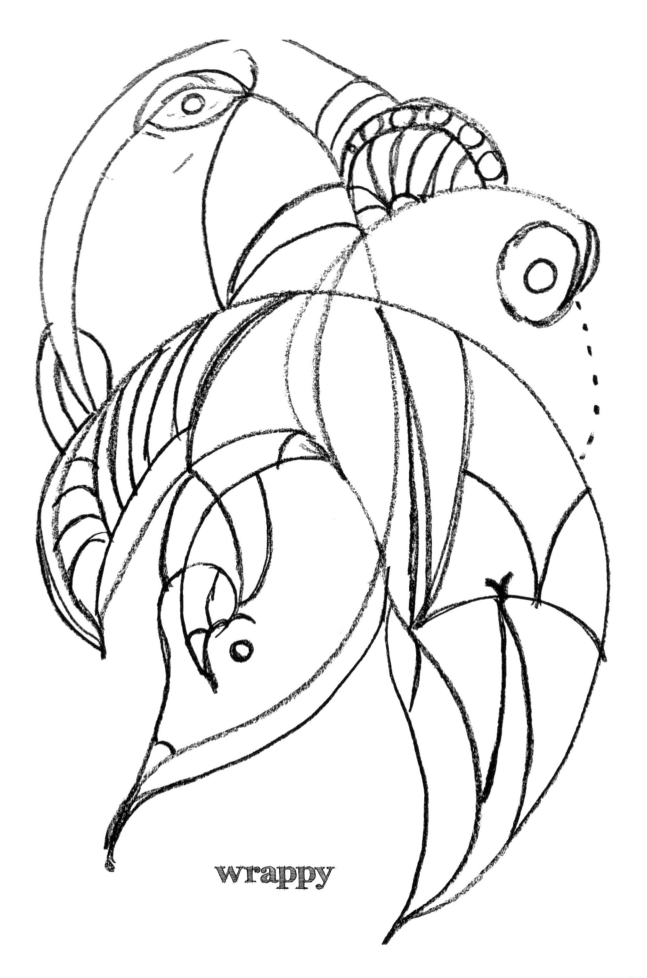

wrappy

Zippy

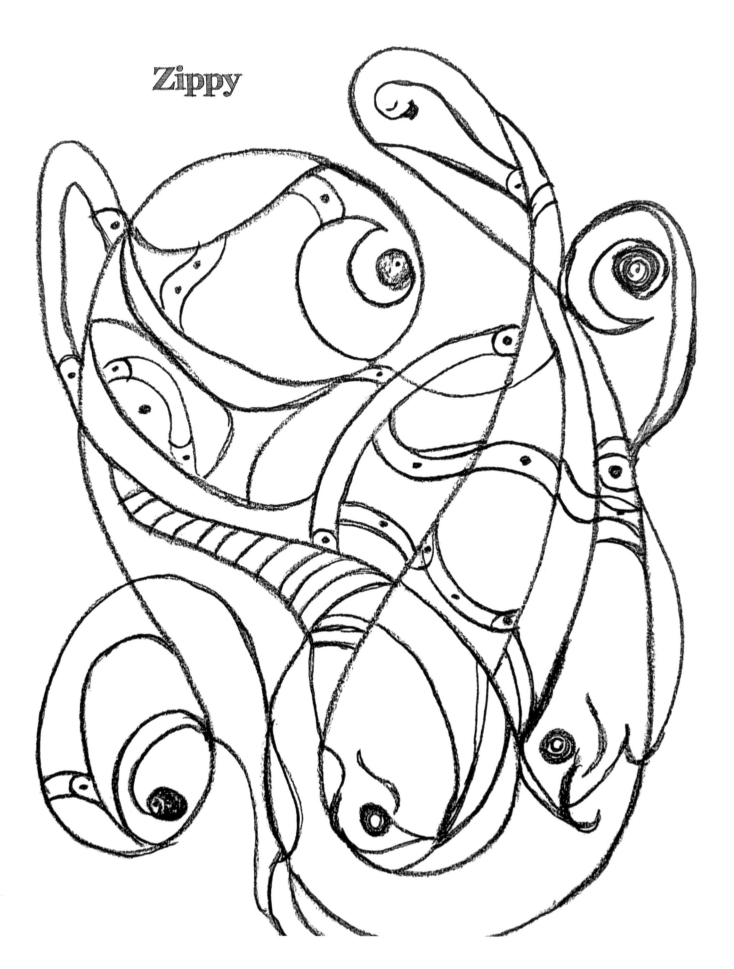

Printed in the United States
by Baker & Taylor Publisher Services